HEINEMANN Profiles

Fidel Castro

An Unauthorized Biography

Petra Press

Heinemann Library
Chicago, Illinois

Published by Heinemann Library, an imprint of Reed Educational & Professional Publishing, 100 N. LaSalle, Suite 1010, Chicago, IL 60602
Customer Service 888-454-2279

Designed by Carney Design
Printed in Hong Kong

04 03 02 01 00
10 9 8 7 6 5 4 3 2 1

Library of Congress Cataloging-in-Publication Data
Press, Petra.
  Fidel Castro : an unauthorized biography / Petra Press.
    p. cm. – (Heinemann profiles)
  Includes bibliographical references (p.) and index.
  Summary: A biography of the president of Cuba, Fidel Castro, discussing his
childhood, family, revolutionary activities, and role as leader of his country since 1959.
  ISBN 1-57572-497-9 (lib. bdg.)
    1. Castro, Fidel, 1927- --Juvenile literature. 2. Cuba—History—1933-1959—Juvenile
literature. 3. Cuba—History 1959- --Juvenile literature. 4.
Revolutionaries—Cuba—Biography—Juvenile literature. 5. Heads of
state—Cuba—Biography—Juvenile literature. [1. Castro, Fidel, 1927-. 2. Heads of state. 3.
Revolutionaries. 4. Cuba—History—1959-] I. Title. II. Series.
F1788.23C3 P74 1999
972.9106'4'092—dc21
[B]   99-051675

Acknowledgments
The Publishers would like to thank the following for permission to reproduce photographs: AP, pp. 4, 15, 17, 44, 47; H. Armstrong Roberts/George Hunter, pp. 7, 11, 18, 24; Sovfoto/Eastphoto, pp. 8, 51; AP/Wide World Photos, pp. 6, 12, 14, 21; Corbis, pp. 13, 29, 35, 36, 37, 43, 49; UPI/Corbis-Bettmann, pp. 19, 23; Woodfin Camp and Associates/Rolando Pujol, p. 26; Eastphoto, p. 30; Corbis/Bettmann-UPI, pp. 31, 32, 33; Sygma/M. Stravato, p. 38; Ulrike Welsch, p. 40; H. Armstrong Roberts/Damm/Zefa, p. 48.

Cover photo: Associated Press

Every effort has been made to contact copyright holders of any material reproduced in this book. Any omissions will be rectified in subsequent printings if notice is given to the Publisher.

Some words are shown in bold, **like this.** You can find out what they mean by looking in the glossary.

This is an unauthorized biography. The subject has not sponsored or endorsed this book.

CONTENTS

Who is Fidel Castro?

Fidel Castro, a controversial leader and revolutionary, took control of the Cuban government in 1959 and has remained firmly in power ever since. Unlike most **dictators** throughout history, Castro achieved widespread loyalty and popularity among his own people, even though he restricted their freedoms of speech and religion. He also turned Cuba into a major player in the **Cold War**.

Fidel Castro's **charisma** has always attracted attention. He still often wears the olive-green uniform of his revolutionary days.

To many Cubans, Castro is a hero who overthrew the **tyrant** Batista and started **socialist** programs that have made health care, housing, and education available to all. To poor and **oppressed** people throughout Latin America and Africa, he became the symbol of **communist** revolution.

To many other people, however, especially the Cubans who have fled his **regime** to the U.S., Castro is a dangerous tyrant. They believe he represses not just personal freedom but also the kind of **capitalistic** growth that could give poor Cubans an opportunity to improve their lives.

Officially, the United States considers Castro a tyrant. For over thirty years, the U.S. government believed that Castro was a threat to American freedom and democracy, because of his alliance with the **USSR.** The result was military confrontation and an economic **embargo.** American anti-Castro policy continues today, and many Cubans believe that it is the U.S. embargo itself, and not Castro, that has been responsible for increasing the poverty of the Cuban people.

Although he is famous for his long speeches, Castro's **idealism** has always been more than just talk. He could have had a successful law practice when he graduated from college, yet chose to use his legal expertise to help the poor. Later, against unbelievable odds, he personally led a handful of Cuban rebels in a bloody fight for freedom that lasted more than six years.

EARLY LIFE

Fidel Alejandro Castro Ruz was born at 2:00 A.M. on August 13, 1926—although some records show 1927—at *Las Manacas,* his father's 23,000-acre (9300-hectare) sugarcane plantation in what was then called Oriente Province. When Fidel was born, it was a poor province in which huge farms were owned either by a privileged few Cuban landowners or by American corporations. The majority of the province's population was made up of desperately poor **tenant farmers** or fishermen who lived in rundown shacks. There was no health care, unemployment was often as high as fifty percent, and many children suffered from **malnutrition.** Most of these peasants could not read or write.

Fidel was one of the lucky few. His father, Angel Castro, was an **illiterate** immigrant who had come to Cuba from Spain in 1905. By working hard, he eventually made enough money to buy land and start his own successful sugar plantation. He also taught himself to read and write. By the time Fidel was born, Angel was a wealthy man, and he wanted his children to have advantages that he had not had. Although Angel remembered his peasant roots, he was often more interested in making a profit than treating his workers fairly.

Oriente Province, where Fidel grew up, was a sprawling area of lush vegetation and rugged hills.

His father's status opened many doors for Fidel, but some people looked down on him because his parents were not married when he was born. Most Cubans were Catholics who considered that a sin. Angel Castro and his first wife, Maria Argota, had two children before 1916. When he became involved with Lina Ruz Gonzalez, a maid in their house who was 25 years younger than he was, Maria divorced him. Over the next several years, although they were not yet married, Lina and Angel had three children—Angela, Ramon, and Fidel. Later, after they married in 1933, she gave birth to four more children—Juana, Raul, Emma, and Augustina.

As the son of a rising landowner, I at least had the advantage of living in the countryside and could mix with the peasants, the humble people, who were all my friends.

Fidel Castro

LIFE ON THE PLANTATION

Fidel had an active early childhood growing up on his father's plantation. The family lived in a large, rambling two-story farmhouse surrounded by dogs and other farm animals. Fidel spent most of his time hunting, fishing, swimming, and riding horseback with his brothers and sisters. He was a very active child, displaying an energy level that would amaze friends and coworkers throughout his life. Fidel also inherited his father's domineering personality and was known to throw temper tantrums when he didn't get his own way.

Because the Castro family lived in one of the most undeveloped regions of Cuba, violence from bandits was always a threat. Angel Castro made sure his children knew how to handle weapons when they were still very young. Fidel learned well and quickly

Young Fidel developed compassion for the poor, hard-working sugarcane cutters who worked on his father's plantation.

Fidel was concerned for the poor even at the age of ten: "I still remember with genuine sorrow how, for example, they [the government under Machado] started to expel the Haitian immigrants who had lived in Cuba for many years. Those Haitians had left their country years before, fleeing from starvation. They grew and cut sugarcane, making great sacrifices, tremendous sacrifices. Their wages were so low they were almost slaves. . . . Nobody cared if they lived or died of starvation."

developed a love of rifles, pistols, shotguns, slingshots, and bows and arrows. While attending high school, he kept a pistol in his room. His skill with guns became valuable later in life, when he became a revolutionary.

Growing up on a large sugar plantation, or *latifundio,* also gave young Fidel experiences that shaped his thoughts and ideals later in life. He befriended sugarcane laborers who endured long hours and terrible working conditions, yet still barely made enough to feed their families, let alone pay for health care and schooling for their children. The children themselves often had to work and never went to school at all. His brother Ramon tells how spending long hours talking with the cane cutters who worked on his dad's farm affected Fidel: "To see children without food, [their parents] without jobs, that makes a man into a rebel."

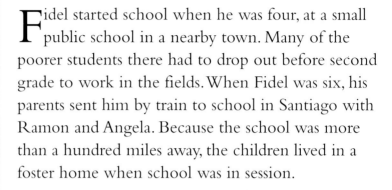

A Rebellious Student

Fidel started school when he was four, at a small public school in a nearby town. Many of the poorer students there had to drop out before second grade to work in the fields. When Fidel was six, his parents sent him by train to school in Santiago with Ramon and Angela. Because the school was more than a hundred miles away, the children lived in a foster home when school was in session.

Fidel was a disruptive student from the beginning, picking fights with other students and throwing tantrums when teachers tried to discipline him. Hoping a stricter school could change Fidel's unruly behavior, his father sent him to the LaSalle school in Santiago at the age of seven. Many wealthy families sent their sons to this **Jesuit**-run school. A year later, his brothers Ramon and Raul joined him. At LaSalle, the boys had to observe a strict dress code, wearing suits and ties.

Because the strict Catholic school would not accept illegitimate children, it was at this time that Fidel's parents finally got married and had their children baptized. Fidel got into almost constant fistfights with students who teased him for having "peasant" parents who had married long after he was born.

Fidel was a bright student whose passion was history. He studied hard and was a perfectionist when it came to his schoolwork. He was also a

talented athlete who **excelled** at soccer, basketball, and baseball throughout his school career.

In 1942, at the age of fifteen, Fidel enrolled at Belen, a famous Jesuit high school in Havana. Instead of looking down on Fidel because of his parents' social class or the circumstances of his birth, the Spanish Jesuit teachers there recognized him at once as a boy with exceptional intelligence and leadership potential. At Belen, Fidel did especially well in history, geography, and debate. He was especially interested in social issues.

During that period I was very active, mainly in sports, the Explorers, and mountain climbing. I did not know—nor could I have imagined then—that I was preparing myself for the revolutionary struggle.

Fidel Castro,
reflecting on his high school years

There had been U.S. businesses in Cuba for years, like this Hershey chocolate factory. Most were concerned with making a profit, not taking care of the Cuban economy.

High School Days

By this time Fidel had become concerned about the poor and **exploited** laborers of Cuba, and their often hopeless living conditions. Although he certainly didn't need to work, Fidel spent his summers driving tractors on his father's plantation, interacting with workers and listening to their concerns. Before he had even entered high school, he began acting on his pro-worker loyalties. At the age of thirteen, he organized his father's own underpaid sugarcane workers to **strike** for higher wages.

Although Angel loved Fidel and gladly paid all his school costs, including his college tuition for law school at the University of Havana, both Angel and Fidel were stubborn people with hot tempers and their relationship was often stormy. Fidel often fought with his father over the family's **"capitalistic"** exploitation of sugar workers, accusing him of "abusing" the workers with "false promises."

In high school, Fidel became interested in national politics. He studied the works of Jose Martí, a leader in Cuba's fight for independence from Spain, and he learned how Cuba had been brutally exploited during the 17th, 18th, and 19th centuries. Fidel was outraged to learn that after winning the Spanish-American War in 1898, American **capitalists** had moved in to exploit Cuban land and labor. When Cuban sugar prices plunged in 1920 from 22 cents per pound to 4 cents per pound, U.S. investors bought up huge tracts of Cuban property at bargain rates. On top of that, during the age of Prohibition in the U.S.—1919 to 1933—Cuba became a favorite vacation spot for wealthy **bootleggers** and celebrities.

Already an excellent debater, Fidel started practicing long and **eloquent** political speeches on his high school classmates. Fidel often quoted his far-sighted revolutionary hero, Jose Martí, who said before he died fighting for Cuban independence in 1895, that Cubans would never be truly free without economic, racial, and sexual equality.

Fidel admired Cuban patriot Jose Martí, who once wrote, "People love liberty, even if they do not know that they love it. They are driven by it and flee from where it does not exist."

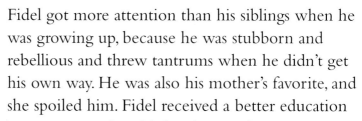

A Changing Cuba

While Fidel was in high school, World War II raged, and Fulgencio Batista became president of Cuba. The war was good to Cuba, mainly because Cuba made a profit supplying the Allies with sugar, nickel, and manganese. In spite of the short outburst of **prosperity** that occurred during his presidency, Batista lost the elections of 1944 to a **socialist** named Dr. Ramon Grau. This was mainly because only the wealthy had profited under Batista, and Grau promised reforms that would benefit the majority of Cubans, who were poor.

Fidel Castro's high school yearbook called him a "distinguished student and a fine athlete."

Fidel got more attention than his siblings when he was growing up, because he was stubborn and rebellious and threw tantrums when he didn't get his own way. He was also his mother's favorite, and she spoiled him. Fidel received a better education than his brothers and sisters. His brother Ramon quit school after the fourth grade because he didn't like it—he preferred living and working on the plantation. The youngest boy, Raul, was as much of a discipline problem as Fidel. Angel and Lina sent him to a military academy when he was five. Fidel didn't go with him only because he stubbornly refused to go to any kind of military school.

Fulgencio Batista, seen here taking the oath of office in 1940, would later become a ruthless and hated dictator—and the target of Fidel's revolution.

Fidel's high school teachers had great hopes for him, as they wrote on his report card: "He won the admiration and affection of all. He will study law, and we have no doubt that he will make a brilliant name for himself. Fidel has what it takes and will make something of himself."

Throughout high school, Fidel remained close to his sister Angela, who attended a girls' school in Santiago. Their father, Angel, became even richer over the years and could have afforded to send them to Santiago or even to Havana. After graduation, Fidel's sisters Emma and Augustina got an apartment together in Havana near the university he attended. Fidel stayed with them off and on while he was in school, especially if he needed a place to hide.

A COLLEGE ACTIVIST

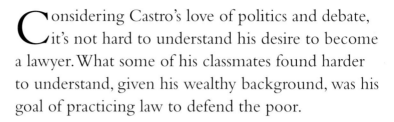

Considering Castro's love of politics and debate, it's not hard to understand his desire to become a lawyer. What some of his classmates found harder to understand, given his wealthy background, was his goal of practicing law to defend the poor.

Castro entered the University of Havana in September of 1945 at the age of 18. He immediately became an important political figure on campus. He talked about politics with his fellow students for hours on end—in class, in coffee shops, and anywhere else he could get them to listen.

Part of Castro's **charisma** during his law school days was his dramatic appearance. Tall, handsome, and self-assured, he usually wore a dark blue suit and tie, already looking the part of an important attorney. Teachers and students all over campus knew who he was and what he stood for. He quickly became a well-known student leader of political groups such as the Students' Directorate and the Generation of 1930. Although **communism** had been around in Cuba since 1925, and although Castro did later become a communist, he was not a communist during his law school days. In fact, he was very anti-communist.

In the fall of 1945, national politics was a hot campus issue for everyone, not just Fidel Castro.

Some Cuban students used violence to make political statements, although in Castro's day, most carried concealed weapons.

President Grau's government was moving away from the promises of social reform that had gotten him elected and was becoming deeply **corrupt.** The Cuban press reported 64 political assassinations and 100 assassination attempts in Cuba during Grau's 1944-1948 term of office.

As one of his former classmates recalls, "He talked politics all the time, all the time, with a very, very grandiose, and at the same time **idealistic** scheme of how to run the country, how to improve things. He did it with a great deal of passion, emotion, and vehemence—convincing people. He had that capacity."

The DuPont
mansion in
Havana was
a symbol
of the
corruption
and foreign
control that
thrived in
Cuba before
Castro's
revolution.

CHOOSING SIDES

In college, Castro joined forces with Eddy Chibas, a
violently anti-**communist** young man. Chibas was a
popular young politician known for his defense of
Cuba's poor against government **corruption** and
exploitation by the rich.

In the spring of 1947, Chibas started a **radical** new
political party called the Cuban People's Party (PCC).
Castro was one of its 100 original members. Publicly,
he campaigned hard to get Chibas elected to
Congress, but his private notes from that time show
that he resented Chibas's power and considered
himself a better leader. But Castro learned a lot from
him. Later, he became one of the party's leading
figures. Like members of other political groups on
campus, Castro helped start a number of violent
demonstrations. He was even accused twice of
murdering opposing student leaders.

Castro and his friends didn't just concentrate on
politics in Cuba. Their idea of helping the poor
and **oppressed** included violently **overthrowing**
repressive governments throughout Latin America.
Above all, they opposed American **imperialism.**

They were not communists. There were communists on campus, but Castro thought they were too conservative—they did not believe the conditions were right for revolution in Latin America.

In 1947, Castro joined a group of 1,200 armed Dominican **exiles** who planned to invade the Dominican Republic and overthrow its hated **dictator**, Rafael Trujillo. The invasion never took place. Trujillo complained to the U.S. government that he was going to be invaded. The U.S. in turn quietly convinced Grau to stop the invasion. The Cuban navy boarded the ship Castro was on before it even got close to the Dominican Republic. Fidel jumped ship to avoid arrest and swam nine miles through shark-infested waters to the Oriente coast. From there he made his way back to Havana and returned to school.

Trujillo's dictatorship of the Dominican Republic finally ended in 1961, when he was assassinated in his car.

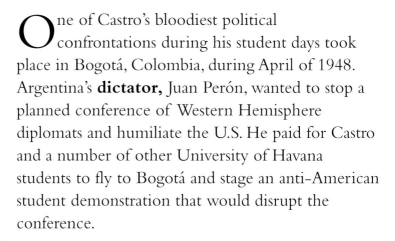

BLOOD IN BOGOTÁ

One of Castro's bloodiest political confrontations during his student days took place in Bogotá, Colombia, during April of 1948. Argentina's **dictator,** Juan Perón, wanted to stop a planned conference of Western Hemisphere diplomats and humiliate the U.S. He paid for Castro and a number of other University of Havana students to fly to Bogotá and stage an anti-American student demonstration that would disrupt the conference.

It was an important conference for the U.S. because the Latin American representatives were there to debate and sign a **treaty** establishing the Organization of American States (OAS). The U.S. said that the OAS would protect Latin America from the spread of **communism.** Perón and other Latin American leaders saw it as a deepening of American **imperialism.** So did the communists. And so did **radical,** pro-labor students like Fidel.

The conference did not begin well. Jorge Gaitan, a leader of the Colombian pro-labor **Liberal** Party, was assassinated before he could give his planned speech. Like Castro and the other Cuban protesters, Gaitan was against **repressive** governments, especially the government in power in Colombia at the time. When he was shot and killed on the sidewalk in front of his office building, everyone blamed everyone else for the assassination.

Bogotá erupted into five days of antigovernment, anti-American street violence. Much of it was triggered by Fidel Castro.

Castro led mobs of angry Colombians into the government's military **armories** to seize guns and tear gas cartridges, then led them into armed confrontation with Bogota's police force. When a photo of Fidel Castro leading the mob made the front page of the Cuban newspapers back home, he became an instant celebrity in his own country.

The Colombian government accused Castro of being a communist troublemaker, even though his actions had nothing to do with communism. To save him from prison or even possible execution, the Cuban **ambassador,** Guillermo Belt, had to smuggle Fidel and the rest of the Cuban students out of the country in a plane carrying cattle.

The riots in Bogota lasted for several days, leaving damaged buildings and overturned streetcars in their wake.

HUSBAND AND FATHER

Politics did not take up all of Fidel's time during his law school years. In the summer of 1948, he married Mirta Diaz–Balart, a pretty, dark–haired **philosophy** student at the University of Havana. She came from a wealthy family that was linked politically to Batista. Fidel met her through her brother Rafael, who also attended the law school. She was his first and only wife.

Mirta's parents were upset to learn that she was marrying a student with a reputation for being a violent **activist.** Fidel's family was much happier about the marriage. Angel paid for an expensive wedding, a long honeymoon in the U.S., and a new car.

After the honeymoon, Fidel was in no hurry to return to Cuba. He and Mirta rented an apartment in New York, where he took a language course to improve his English. He briefly thought about studying at Columbia University, but he changed his mind. It was politics that lured him back to Cuba.

The couple moved into a small, inexpensive hotel room in downtown Havana, where they lived for a year. In September 1949, Mirta had a child the couple named Felix Fidel Castro Diaz—"Fidelito" for short. Although Fidel loved his son dearly, he spent so much time involved with classes and politics that he was seldom at home.

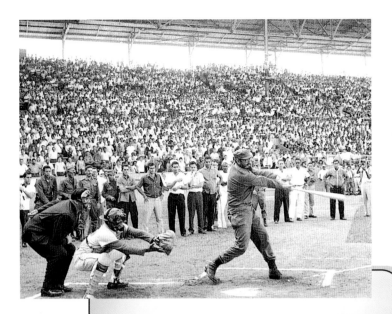

After coming to power, Fidel Castro could often be seen at baseball games, throwing out the first pitch or even taking a few swings.

Fidel's love of baseball continued to grow during his university years—and so did his talent as a pitcher. There are stories that he was so good that he was scouted by at least two major-league clubs before he graduated in 1950, and that he even turned down an offer—including a $5,000 signing bonus— from the New York Giants. He preferred to remain an amateur, he said, and wanted to complete his studies. Many historians have often wondered how the second half of the twentieth century would have turned out if Castro had accepted the Giants' offer, although others do not believe that the stories are true.

BATISTA COMES BACK

Fidel graduated from law school in 1950 at the age of 23 and opened a law practice for the poor, as he had intended. He quickly got involved in social work, refusing to take any money from his poor clients, and continued to be active in Havana politics.

The government of President Prío Socarrás, which came into power in the 1948 elections, had become just as **corrupt** as Grau's had been before him. The very anti-Prío PCC—Cuban **Liberal** Party—was gaining support. Fulgencio Batista had to move fast. In March of 1952, before new elections could take

After Batista moved back into the Presidential Palace, he canceled all elections and suspended Cuba's constitution.

place, he took control of the government in a bloodless **coup.** With the help of a group of junior army officers, Batista waited until a weekend in March when many government officials were away on reelection campaigns. At 2:30 in the morning, he and his rebel officers walked into the presidential quarters and arrested the soldiers there.

Other officers took over the national telephone company and all of the the radio and television stations. No one was killed; no one even offered any resistance. By 5:00 A.M. the operation was complete. When news of the takeover reached President Prío, he tried to get support from other army posts, but he was not able to find anyone who was willing to oppose Batista.

Under Batista's new **dictatorship,** social conditions in Cuba went from bad to worse. By 1953, more than 600,000 Cubans were unemployed and about 3.5 million people (over half of Cuba's population) lived in **slums** without electricity. Disease was widespread and health care was poor. Economic and social **discrimination** against blacks and other minorities was not only common, but legal.

Under Batista, corruption and foreign control thrived. The most **prosperous** industries in Cuba were owned by American companies, and only about one percent of the money they made filtered down to the Cuban people. Between government corruption and the U.S. economic control over Cuba, little was left for the Cuban people.

GETTING RID OF BATISTA

At first, immediately following Batista's successful **coup,** Castro tried a non-violent, legal approach— he asked the Cuban courts to declare Batista's government to be illegal. He lost. When the legal approach failed, he turned to violence and started planning a revolution. He and his followers devoted months to military training. They studied the ideas of Jose Martí and made plans to supply their followers with weapons and to get financial support.

In response to public pressure, Castro was released from prison in 1955. Batista believed he was no longer a threat.

On July 26, 1953, Castro and 100 others attacked the Moncada army **barracks** near Santiago de Chile. Their mission was to get guns for future attacks against Batista. They also hoped to spark the Cuban people into a revolutionary fever. The attack was crushed by the military, and Castro was captured. Most of his followers were tortured and killed. At his trial three months later, Castro delivered a short but heroic speech that ended with the phrase "la historia me absolvera"—history will absolve me. He was sentenced to 15 years in prison.

While he was in prison, Castro read constantly, especially authors such as Marx and Lenin. He and his followers traded coded messages about their revolutionary plans by

> Then one day a copy of [Karl Marx's] Communist **Manifesto** fell into my hands. What phrases! What truths! . . . When I saw the origin of human society and its class divisions, it was so convincing that it hit me like a clap of thunder . . .

hiding them in cigars. He wrote entire pamphlets, which were sent this way and then published.

Fidel also wrote letters. Some were to his wife Mirta and his young son Fidelito, who had just turned four. He was always anxious about how and what his son was doing, but he didn't seem to miss Mirta much. His letters to her were not filled with much affection. When he found out that she had taken a job with Batista's government after he was put in prison, he was so angry that he filed for divorce, even though she had written letters to the editors of Havana newspapers pleading for public support for her husband's release. Shortly after the divorce became final in 1955, Mirta went to live in Spain. She never talks about her marriage.

Mirta was not the only woman in Fidel's life while he was in prison. He also wrote letters to a wealthy and beautiful married woman named Natalia Revuelta. Castro had met her in the early fifties when her prorevolutionary sympathy led her to invite Castro and his supporters to use her house as a meeting place. They shared a love of politics and **philosophy.**

EXILE IN MEXICO

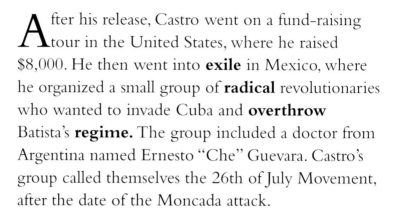

After his release, Castro went on a fund-raising tour in the United States, where he raised $8,000. He then went into **exile** in Mexico, where he organized a small group of **radical** revolutionaries who wanted to invade Cuba and **overthrow** Batista's **regime.** The group included a doctor from Argentina named Ernesto "Che" Guevara. Castro's group called themselves the 26th of July Movement, after the date of the Moncada attack.

Their ideas were based on a 15-point **manifesto** written by Castro. For the first time, he began seriously to consider Marx and Lenin's **communist** ideas. His revolutionary program called for the distribution of land to peasants; the right of workers to share in the profits generated by Cuba's industrial, commercial, and mining enterprises; construction of cheap, decent housing for poor urban families; educational opportunities and health care for everyone regardless of income or social status; an end to all racial and sexual **discrimination**; and other social and economic reforms to make life better for the Cuban people.

Being in exile in Mexico didn't keep Castro from fighting to see his son. He persuaded Mirta to let Fidelito visit him in 1955, accompanied by his two aunts, Emma and Augustina. He told Mirta that he might not survive the revolution to see his son again. Shortly after that, the boy was kidnapped from his aunts in Mexico City and returned to his mother in Havana. Mirta then took the boy to live in New York for a year, where he attended school.

In 1956, Castro learned that Natalia Revuelta, who had written to him in prison, was pregnant with his child. Nati, as he called her, was married to a heart specialist named Orlando Fernandez at the time, but in March she had a daughter named Alina. Although Nati was very much in love with Fidel, she did not divorce her husband. She continued to be a friend to Castro, although after 1956, he devoted almost all of his attention to the revolution.

Alina took the last name of Fernandez, even though it was no secret that she was Castro's daughter. Over the years, Castro visited his daughter as often as he could during his revolutionary campaign. But in the autobiography she published in 1977, Alina complained bitterly about years of neglect.

Fidel persuaded Mirta to let Fidelito visit him while he was exiled in Mexico.

THE REVOLUTION

Castro and his 80 followers returned to Cuba in December of 1956 on a boat named *Granma*. Their landing on the coast of Oriente Province was an almost total disaster. Not only had Batista's government learned about their arrival, but bad weather and miscommunication prevented Castro's supporters from showing up in time to give them back-up. Batista's troops killed all but twelve of them.

In spite of their huge losses, the survivors—who included Fidel, his brother Raul, and Che Guevara—continued their fight. For two years they used the Sierra Maestra mountains as their base of operations and, using **guerrilla** warfare, were able to humiliate Batista's forces with hundreds of attacks on small army posts.

Castro's army was made up of farmers and workers from small towns. Castro and his band trained them in the use of weapons.

Castro also waged a highly effective **propaganda** campaign. In addition to distributing pamphlets, he took over a radio station in the spring of 1958. Radio Rebelde broadcast his promises to restore Cuba's constitution, eliminate government **corruption,** hold free elections, improve educational systems, and

Friends in High Places

Castro rewarded his followers with positions in his new government. Brother Raul became Minister of the Armed Forces. Che Guevara helped organize agricultural and industrial reforms in Cuba. He was later killed in Bolivia, where he was helping to lead a revolution. Camilo Cienfuegos became a military commander but disappeared in late 1959 in a plane at sea. Celia Sanchez became Castro's assistant and secretary.

Five weeks after his forces rode triumphantly into Havana, Castro reinstated Cuba's constitution.

provide national health care. To the poor people of Cuba, these promises were very appealing.

With the help of growing numbers of volunteers throughout the island, Castro's forces won a string of victories. By December of 1959, Castro's army had grown to almost 2,000 members. Incredibly, this small band was getting the better of Batista's 30,000-man professional army. On January 1, 1959, Castro's revolutionary forces took control of Havana.

Cuba Goes Communist

After declaring Cuba to be a Communist country in 1961, Castro set an example by helping with the annual sugarcane harvest.

The revolution created not just a new government, but a whole new Cuban society that included massive social and economic reforms. Castro started by **nationalizing** all American-owned businesses and industries, declaring that it was in the best interests of the Cuban people.

Next, he called for major land reforms that nationalized all farms larger than 1,000 acres (400 hectares). The land was then split up. Some was given to workers and peasants in 67-acre (27-hectare) parcels to be farmed individually. Some was made into cooperatives in which the peasants did not own the land but farmed it as a group.

Castro also outlawed all religion, including Catholicism, Cuba's main religion. The Catholic church, which had been a major influence in Cuban politics and education, now had no power at all.

Castro immediately started setting up a free health care system for all Cuban citizens. He also made education free to everyone,

from kindergarten through university study. He started a huge public works program, hiring workers to build new hospitals, schools, roads, and clinics. Racial **discrimination** was officially made illegal.

Such reform measures did not come without a price, however. Freedom of speech was ended, and anti-Castro **dissidents** were put in jail or executed without a trial. The government controlled not only newspapers, but also all television and radio programming. Travel permits to leave Cuba became very hard to get.

While Castro's new policies were appealing to the majority of Cubans—the poor—many middle and upper class Cubans were horrified by his reforms. They fled in large numbers to the United States. Not just former business and landowners who lost their money and property left, but also professional people. By 1961, Cuba had lost half of its doctors and teachers.

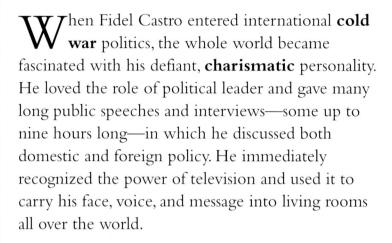

THE COLD WAR

When Fidel Castro entered international **cold war** politics, the whole world became fascinated with his defiant, **charismatic** personality. He loved the role of political leader and gave many long public speeches and interviews—some up to nine hours long—in which he discussed both domestic and foreign policy. He immediately recognized the power of television and used it to carry his face, voice, and message into living rooms all over the world.

Soviet leader Nikita Khrushchev met Castro while attending the 15th anniversary of the founding of the United Nations in New York in 1960. He immediately saw Cuba's rebel hero as a potentially powerful voice for **communism** in Latin America. He also realized that Cuba's location—just 90 miles from the **USSR's** main enemy, the United States—could be useful. The U.S. saw this alliance as a threat to national security.

In the first year after he came to power, Castro was careful not to stay in one place too long. He used the 23rd floor of a Havana hotel as both his home and office, as well a house in a fishing village five miles out of the city, the apartment of his friend and official assistant, Celia Sanchez, and an office in a government building. He especially liked to work while he was being driven around from one place to another in three-car motorcades of Oldsmobiles full of bodyguards carrying guns. Sometimes even Celia didn't know exactly where he was. In later years, he moved into the Presidential Palace, but he never slowed down.

> He was the kind of person who couldn't be ignored. If he was in a room, people paid attention to him.
>
> Natalia Revuelta, mother of Castro's daughter, Alina Fernandez.

Castro had refused to stay in an expensive hotel in New York, but Khrushchev visited him in his room in the **slums** of Harlem in 1960.

THE U.S. STEPS IN

April of 1961 brought a turning point in **Cold War diplomacy.** The United States was beginning to regard Cuba, with its strategic location just 90 miles off the Florida coast and its ties to **USSR,** as a serious security threat. The Central Intelligence Agency **(CIA)** resolved to bring the Castro **regime** down.

The CIA secretly equipped and trained 1,500 Cuban **exiles** to invade Cuba at a spot on its coastline called Playa Giron, or the Bay of Pigs. Worried that other nations would be angry with the U.S. if they suspected U.S. involvement, President Kennedy decided at the last minute not to send fighter planes to protect the invading troops. As a result, the invaders were defeated by the Cuban army and the United States was publicly humiliated.

The U.S. had to agree to send $50 million of equipment in exchange for the release of the

President Kennedy and his wife speak to survivors of the Bay of Pigs invasion. Cuban exiles had pressured the U.S. government to act against Castro.

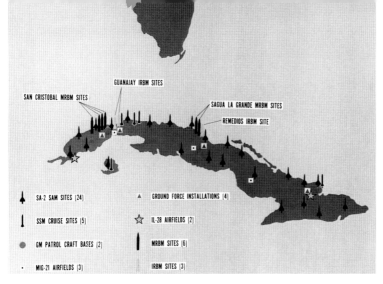

GUANAJAY IRBM SITES

SAN CRISTOBAL MRBM SITES

SAGUA LA GRANDE MRBM SITES

REMEDIOS IRBM SITE

SA-2 SAM SITES (24)

SSM CRUISE SITES (5)

GM PATROL CRAFT BASES (2)

MIG-21 AIRFIELDS (3)

GROUND FORCE INSTALLATIONS (4)

IL-28 AIRFIELDS (2)

MRBM SITES (6)

IRBM SITES (3)

By allowing the USSR to place missiles in Cuba aimed at the U.S., Castro brought the world to the brink of nuclear war.

Cuban-Americans who had been captured. After the failed invasion, Castro declared: "the **imperialists** cannot forgive that we have made a **socialist** revolution under the nose of the United States."

Cuba soon began acquiring weapons from the USSR, which had become the nation's chief financial supporter and trade partner. In October of 1962, the CIA informed President Kennedy that the USSR had secretly stationed 42 medium-range **nuclear** missiles in Cuba that could be aimed at American cities. Kennedy demanded that the USSR withdraw the missiles. He also sent U.S. Navy ships to Cuba to prevent any additional shipments of **Soviet** arms.

The world held its breath. The world's two most powerful nations were on the brink of nuclear war. The crisis ended when the Soviet Union agreed to withdraw its nuclear weapons from Cuba, in exchange for a promise that the U.S. would no longer try to **overthrow** Castro's regime. Publically, the U.S. government agreed. Secretly, the CIA created Operation Mongoose, another Cuban invasion force, with 2,000 agents and a budget of $50 million to support small-scale attacks on the Cuban coast.

ECONOMIC EMBARGO

Over the years, in spite of his **communist** and pro-**Soviet** leanings, and in spite of confrontations like the Bay of Pigs disaster and the Cuban Missile Crisis, Castro has repeatedly declared that he is willing to renew diplomatic relations with the United States. His condition is that the U.S. must end its trade **embargo** against Cuba. Not only has the U.S. refused his offer, but in recent years, Cuban–Americans who fled Castro's revolution have gained enough support in Congress to call for even stronger measures. They point to the **rafters** as proof that Castro's revolution has failed.

The UN estimates that only three of every four rafters who leave Cuba ever make it to Florida.

> They don't have to put me in jail. The whole country is a jail.
>
> Elizardo Sanchez,
> Cuban **dissident**

In the past few years, thousands of Cubans have died trying to leave their country for a better life in the U.S., many of them on unsafe homemade rafts, often made out of inner tubes or foam rubber.

Cuban rafters made up the Mariel Freedom Flotilla in 1980, when Castro opened the Cuban port of Mariel and allowed Cubans to leave. President Jimmy Carter had U.S. ships pick up some 125,000 Cubans from the port, thinking they were political **refugees.** It was not until later that it was discovered that among these refugees were a large number of hardened criminals.

Rafting reached new heights in the early 1990s. Over 3,500 Cubans made it to Florida in 1993. By the summer of 1994, over 2,000 people a day were trying to get there. Today, Cubans are treated like any other people who want to come to the U.S. The U.S. government has set a limit of 20,000 Cubans to move to the U.S. every year, and warns Cubans that they must go through the official application process.

The poor are not the only people who have been trying to flee Cuba. Athletes, musicians, artists, and even government officials have left.

END THE EMBARGO?

Castro continues to blame the U.S. **embargo** for his country's devastating poverty and crippled economy. Much of the world today agrees with him. In 1998, for the sixth year in a row, the UN General Assembly debated a **resolution** calling for an end to the embargo. Of the 146 countries that voted on the Cuban-sponsored resolution, only three—the United States, Israel and Uzbekistan—voted against. In 1999, a bipartisan group of U.S. senators started working to end restrictions on the sale of food and medicine to the island. U.S. business interests are also urging the president to begin easing the embargo.

In spite of increasing world pressure to end the embargo, in early 1995, the U.S. Congress passed a law strengthening it. The Cuban Democracy Act not only forbids American companies from doing business in or trading with Cuba, it also seeks to penalize foreign companies who trade with Cuba.

Many Americans have defended the bill as being in the best interests of the Cuban people. The strong Cuban-American community in the U.S. and many other supporters of the embargo believe that

In Cuba, many basic foods are rationed, although in some places land is now being given to individuals to farm.

Hard to Kill

Fidel has survived more than 30 assassination attempts over the past forty years, most of them by the American **CIA.** Starting in August 1960, the CIA has tried poisoned cigars, exploding cigars, inserts in his shoes that would make his hair fall out, and a scuba diving suit infected with tuberculosis bacteria. They have even hired men to try to shoot Castro. Not one of the attempts has been successful. "I should be awarded a medal," says Castro, "because there is no individual against whom so many assassination plots have been contrived, who is still living."

Castro's **human rights** abuses have been so extreme over the years that even though it has not hurt his hold on the Cuban government so far, the embargo must continue because it will bring him down eventually.

I am profoundly convinced what we have been doing is the fair thing to do. It is the noblest thing to do and the most humane, and we will never be **repentant** for that. Never.

Fidel Castro, defending his revolution, 1995

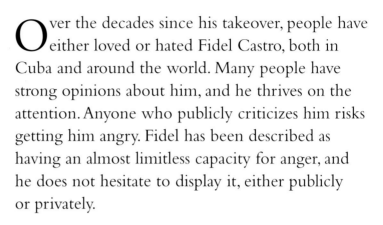

THE MANY FACES OF FIDEL

Over the decades since his takeover, people have either loved or hated Fidel Castro, both in Cuba and around the world. Many people have strong opinions about him, and he thrives on the attention. Anyone who publicly criticizes him risks getting him angry. Fidel has been described as having an almost limitless capacity for anger, and he does not hesitate to display it, either publicly or privately.

Back in his revolutionary days in the Sierra Maestra, he would fly into a rage if one of his **guerrillas** wasted even a single bullet. As president, it has been common for him to swear and throw a fit over the smallest mistake. Even people who have been with him since the revolution are afraid of his anger.

From the day he took control of Cuba in 1959, Castro has kept up an incredible pace of activity. Until he was in his sixties, he would go to bed at three or four in the morning, yet look fresh and rested at 9:00 A.M. conferences. When working on a particular project, he could go without sleep for over forty hours at a time, taking short naps in a small bedroom behind his office.

Over the years Castro has also become known as a perfectionist, spending hours correcting and rewriting his lengthy speeches until his words are not just meaningful but elegant.

People who have met Castro have described him as a strange mixture of beautiful manners and surprising rudeness. When women are present he can be soft-spoken and courteous, but when he is alone with men, he doesn't hesitate to swear, treat servants badly, or even spit on the floor. He has an almost regal bearing in meetings and interviews, yet doesn't seem concerned when bits of food get caught in his beard while he is eating with guests.

One of Castro's projects has been to provide free education to all children in Cuba.

The American writer Ernest Hemingway lived in Cuba for years. He met Castro at a fishing contest.

PRIVATE LIFE

Although Castro has remained a baseball fan over the years, work has left little time to enjoy sports. Usually, the few times during the year when Castro takes a vacation, he flies with a few friends to the seaside town of Cayo Piedra, where he engages in one of his favorite sports— underwater fishing. Dinner on these outings usually consists of his catches of the day: turtle soup, lobster, and baked red snapper.

FAMILY SUPPORT

The majority of Cuban people have supported Castro's ongoing **communist** revolution over the last four decades because he has given them what he promised—health care, education, and jobs. Publicly, most of his family has supported him as well. Although Raul sometimes disagrees with Fidel privately about government policies, he has remained publicly loyal to him and is still his second in command. The only family member who openly disagreed with Fidel was his sister Juana. When he proclaimed himself a communist, she moved to Mexico and had no further contact with him.

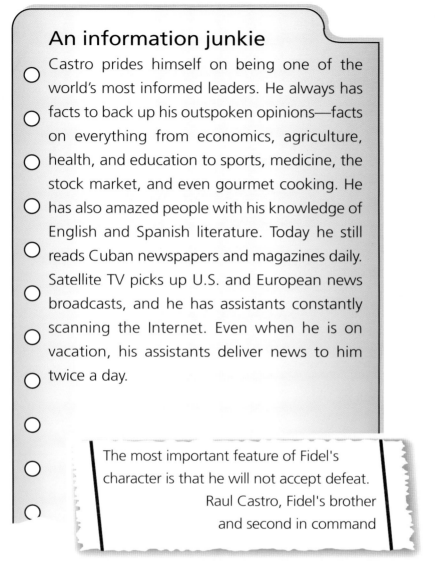

An information junkie

Castro prides himself on being one of the world's most informed leaders. He always has facts to back up his outspoken opinions—facts on everything from economics, agriculture, health, and education to sports, medicine, the stock market, and even gourmet cooking. He has also amazed people with his knowledge of English and Spanish literature. Today he still reads Cuban newspapers and magazines daily. Satellite TV picks up U.S. and European news broadcasts, and he has assistants constantly scanning the Internet. Even when he is on vacation, his assistants deliver news to him twice a day.

The most important feature of Fidel's character is that he will not accept defeat.

Raul Castro, Fidel's brother and second in command

Castro has not been involved with anyone romantically since his marriage to Mirta ended in 1955 and his affair with Natalia Revuelta ended several years later. However, Celia Sanchez was a constant friend and companion, from the days when she fought with him during the revolution to her job as his assistant, until her death from cancer in 1980.

CASTRO MEETS THE POPE

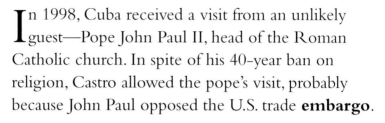

In 1998, Cuba received a visit from an unlikely guest—Pope John Paul II, head of the Roman Catholic church. In spite of his 40-year ban on religion, Castro allowed the pope's visit, probably because John Paul opposed the U.S. trade **embargo**.

In addition to criticizing the U.S. embargo, John Paul pleased Castro by speaking out against **capitalism,** saying it dehumanizes people and limits the economic development of society's poorest members. "True freedom," he said, includes "the recognition of **human rights** and social justice." He also spoke out for freedom of speech and greater religious freedom, especially for the Catholic Church.

Each man gained a lot by the meeting. For Castro, the visit of the pope and the easing of religious bans softened the world's opinion of him. It also won him renewed support from Cubans who missed the comforts of religion. "The revolution always offered health, education, sports, but nothing for the spirit," said one young Cuban. Pope John Paul added the achievement of preaching peace and freedom in a practicing **communist** state to his legacy.

Perhaps in their discussions, Fidel Castro and Pope John Paul II realized that their philosophies are not so different, after all. They both share a deep concern for the welfare of the world's poor, as well as the belief that people everywhere have a responsibility

Castro's warm welcome of the pope surprised many of his critics.

No Room for Religion

When Castro outlawed religion in 1959 as part of his Revolution, Cuba had been primarily Roman Catholic for nearly five centuries. But communist **philosophy** opposes religion because it keeps people distracted from the need to change the terrible conditions so many people face. Also, the Catholic church had a lot of political power in Cuba, which Castro saw as a threat to his rule.

to help the less fortunate. Castro showed respect for John Paul, while the pope extended "paternal warmth" to one who is a long-lapsed Catholic.

Since the Pope's visit, Castro has gradually eased restrictions on the church, and in December of 1998 he recognized Christmas as a holiday in his country for the first time in years.

O n January 1, 1999, Fidel Castro celebrated the 40th anniversary of the day that he and his followers defeated the hated **dictator** Batista. About 1,000 Cuban leaders, celebrities, and foreign diplomats chanted "Fidel! Fidel!" as Castro returned to the square in Havana where he proclaimed his revolution 40 years ago. He was still wearing his trademark beard and military uniform.

Castro has outlasted the collapse of the **USSR,** not to mention surviving countless assassination attempts and decades of U.S. hostility. His rule is still absolute, and hundreds of political prisoners are still in Cuban jails. **Refugees** continue to flee, and groups of anti-Castro revolutionaries continue to plot his **overthrow.** Yet somehow Castro has managed to endure it all.

He is a little more organized than in the days of the revolution, but he still hates schedules and bureaucracy. He is also still a family man who values his privacy. In 1963, Fidel spoke at his mother Lina's funeral. It was the last time he commented on his

Many of Fidel's comrades, like Che Guevara and Camilo Cienfuegos, have died, but the Revolution lives on.

private life in public. His ex-wife Mirta remarried in Spain when their son Fidelito was still young. But Fidelito returned to Cuba to study **nuclear** engineering at the University of Havana. Castro later appointed him head of Cuba's Atomic Energy Commission.

We're talkin' baseball

On March 29, 1999, after long negotiations, the Baltimore Orioles played a Cuban all-star team in Havana. Cuba didn't win, but they played well. Fifty thousand spectators saw the game, including Castro himself. It was the first appearance by a major league club in Cuba in forty years. There was a rematch in Baltimore the following May, which Cuba won.

Cubans continue to protest the U.S. embargo, which has restricted supplies of food, gas, clothing, and medicine.

CASTRO'S LEGACY

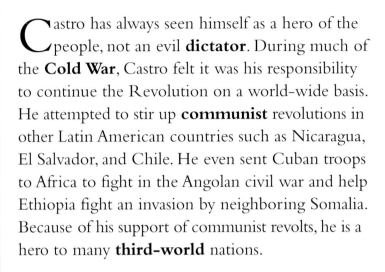

Castro has always seen himself as a hero of the people, not an evil **dictator**. During much of the **Cold War**, Castro felt it was his responsibility to continue the Revolution on a world-wide basis. He attempted to stir up **communist** revolutions in other Latin American countries such as Nicaragua, El Salvador, and Chile. He even sent Cuban troops to Africa to fight in the Angolan civil war and help Ethiopia fight an invasion by neighboring Somalia. Because of his support of communist revolts, he is a hero to many **third-world** nations.

The U.S. responded to the spread of communism in the 1960s by creating the Alliance for Progress Program. This program provided economic aid, military supplies, and training for antirevolutionary, anticommunist forces throughout Latin America. In the 1980s, Presidents Reagan and Bush continued to use the **CIA** to fight communism in countries such as Chile, Nicaragua, and El Salvador.

During the Cold War, the **USSR** saw Castro as a leader who could spread communism through Latin America. Although that didn't happen, they supported Cuba for years, until their collapse in 1991 cost Cuba $6 billion in annual **subsidies.** Castro found that he had to make up for the loss by allowing some **free-market** activities, but Cuba remained the only communist country in the Western Hemisphere. It also became one of the poorest.

Even after the end of the Cold War, Fidel Castro remains a controversial figure.

To some Cubans, Castro is the hero who gave them free education, free health care, and the chance to get away from the **oppression** of American **imperialism**. To others, he is a ruthless dictator who has restricted personal freedom and ruined Cuba's economy.

In recent years, the U.S. has been under increasing pressure—from both the international community and American businesses—to end the **embargo** that is devastating the Cuban people. But many Cuban **refugees** who now live in the U.S. do not want to abandon their homeland. They continue to pressure the U.S. government to remove Castro from power. But Castro is now in his seventies, and a whole new generation has grown up since his revolution took place. It might be simply a matter of outlasting him.

Don't worry about elections. I'm not interested in staying in power one minute more than necessary.
>   Fidel Castro, speaking to "Meet the Press"
>   three months after the revolution in 1959

FIDEL CASTRO–TIMELINE

1926	Fidel Alejandro Castro Ruz born on August 13
1930	Starts grade school
1934	Fulgencio Batista takes over the Cuban government
1940	The Constitution of 1940 is established; General Batista is officially elected president
1942	Enrolls in a **Jesuit** high school in Havana
1943-4	Named the best high school athlete in Cuba
1944	Ramon Grau is elected president
1945	Graduates high school; enrolls at University of Havana; Cuba joins United Nations
1947	Joins a group of Dominican **exiles** in attempt to **overthrow** Dictator Trujillo
1948	Carlos Prío Socarrás elected president; Fulgencio Batista elected to the Cuban Senate Castro participates in Colombia's Bogotazo riots Marries Mirta Diaz-Balart
1949	Son Felix Fidel "Fidelito" Castro Ruz born
1950	Graduates law school and opens his own practice; makes his first trip to New York
1951	Nominated as candidate for Cuban Congress
1952	Fulgencio Batista takes over (again) in a bloodless **coup**; elections are canceled Castro petitions Cuban courts to have Batista's dictatorial government declared illegal; he fails
1953	Leads failed attack on Moncada army **barracks;** arrested and sentenced to 15 years in prison
1955	Released from prison; leaves for Mexico where he forms revolutionary group
1956	March: Daughter Alina Revuelta Fernandez born

	October: Travels to U.S. to raise funds
	December 2: disastrous attack on Oriente coast; survivors escape to nearby mountains
1957	Launches **guerrilla** warfare against Batista
1959	January 1: Revolutionary forces take control of Havana; Batista and his family flee; Cuba's Constitution of 1940 is reinstated; Castro **nationalizes** U.S. companies
1960	U.S. imposes **embargo**; Castro increasingly allies himself with **USSR**
1961	Officially declares himself a **Marxist–Leninist;** U.S. breaks **diplomatic** ties with Cuba April: Bay of Pigs Invasion
1962	Cuban Missile Crisis
1980	President Carter approves Mariel Boat Lift of 125,000 **refugees**
1987	U.S. and Cuba sign new immigration **treaty;** Castro breaks agreement after five months
1991	USSR splits up; aid to Cuba ends
1994	Rafting increases; over 2,000 Cubans a day head for Florida coast
1995	U.S. passes Helms–Burton Act that forbids American companies from doing business in or trading with Cuba
1996	Castro orders Cuban MIG fighters to shoot down two planes owned by Cuban exile organization
1998	UN General Assembly calls for an end to the embargo; 143 countries support the **resolution** Pope John Paul visits Cuba; Castro loosens religious restrictions
1999	Cuba celebrates 40th anniversary of Revolution; Cuban baseball team plays Baltimore Orioles

GLOSSARY

activist person who actively works for change

ambassador person who lives in a country in order to represent his or her own country

armory place where weapons are stored

barracks buildings for housing soldiers

bootlegger someone who made or sold liquor between 1920 and 1933, when it was illegal in the U.S.

capitalism economic system in which most land and business are privately owned

Central Intelligence Agency (CIA) U.S. government agency that protects the nation's security

charisma special quality of leadership that inspires loyalty and devotion

Cold War period after World War II of unfriendly relations (yet no actual warfare) between the U.S. and communist countries

communism social and economic system in which all property and goods are owned by the government

corrupt dishonest

coup sudden takeover of a government by a small group

dictator ruler with complete power not answerable to a parliament

diplomacy keeping up relations between different countries

discrimination treating some people or groups of people in an unfair way

dissident person who disagrees with the government in power

economic blockade government order that forbids trade with a certain country; also called an embargo

eloquent expressed well

embargo government order that forbids trade with a certain country

excel to do very well at something

exile someone who is living in another country because of being forced to leave his or her native country

exploit to take unfair advantage of someone or something

free-market economic system with very few government restrictions on trade

guerrilla warfare using small attacks rather than large battles; a person who fights this way

human rights basic rights that belong to all people

idealism practice of forming ideals and living by them

illiterate unable to read or write

imperialism system in which one country has power over another

Jesuit Roman Catholic religious order devoted to missionary work and education

liberal believing in progress and individual rights

malnutrition not well fed

manifesto written statement of beliefs and ideas

Marxist-Leninist believer in the communist ideas developed by Vladimir Lenin from the writings of Karl Marx

nationalize to place property or business under government control

nuclear using atomic energy

oppress to rule in a harsh way

overthrow to cause the fall of a government

philosophy study of ideas about knowledge and values

propaganda organized spreading of certain ideas

prosperity wealth

radical favoring rapid, extreme changes in law and government

rafter person who flees Cuba by boat or raft, hoping to cross the 90 miles of ocean to Florida

ration to control the amount of something that someone can use, such as food

refugee person who flees from his or her home or country to seek shelter elsewhere

regime system of government in power

repression prevention of the expression of ideas or beliefs that do not agree with government policy

resolution decision passed by vote in the United Nations

slum very poor area of a city

socialism social system in which the production and distribution of goods are controlled by the people

Soviet having to do with the USSR

strike to refuse to work, usually as a group, until certain demands are met

subsidies money granted by one government to another

tenant farmer someone who farms land owned by another person, usually in exchange for a share of the crop

Third World the underdeveloped countries of the world

treaty signed agreement between two or more nations

tyrant ruler who has total power and often uses it harshly

USSR (also called the Soviet Union) communist country which included Russia and other nations. It split up in 1991.

INDEX

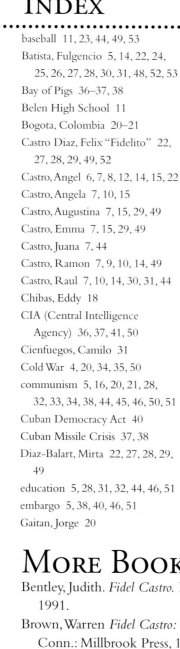

MORE BOOKS TO READ

Bentley, Judith. *Fidel Castro.* Parsippany, N.J.: Silver Burdett Press, 1991.

Brown, Warren *Fidel Castro: Cuban Revolutionary.* Brookfield, Conn.: Millbrook Press, 1994.

Clinton, Susan. *The Cuban Missile Crisis.* Danbury, Conn: Children's Press, 1993.

Rice, Earl Jr. *The Cuban Revolution.* San Diego: Lucent Books, 1995.